'This is the perfect book to help us all celebrat
care of the world Jesus entered into. No need to
through the maze. So get reading and get on wit
Dr Ruth Valerio, environmentalist, theologian,

'Grounded in biblical wisdom and filled with practical ideas, this book serves as a catalyst for conversations about creating a slower approach to Christmas with more time for what truly matters. So when the shops start to fill with stuff we don't need, the true cost of which we can't see, dare to dream that there is another, greener way. Make a cuppa and start here…'
Helen Stephens, church relations manager, A Rocha UK

'Have you ever longed to do Christmas differently but not been sure how to make the change? If so, this wonderful book is just for you. Olivia will help you to declutter your Christmas of unsustainable (and often stressful) features, to fill it with more simplicity, joy and laughter.'
The Revd Margot R. Hodson, director of theology and education, The John Ray Initiative

'Packed full of practical suggestions, and rooted in biblical wisdom, Olivia has managed to help us think about greening our Christmases without lots of handwringing or guilt. This is a highly accessible guide, especially for busy households, which will give you the confidence to take action. As she says, we can't do everything. But we can do THIS.'
Sarah Edwards, executive director, JustMoney Movement (justmoney.org.uk)

'This book is brimming with inspiration and tips to help you reduce your impact on the planet at Christmas, while having fun and pausing to reflect on the "reason for the season". Highly recommended!'
Caroline Pomeroy, director, Climate Stewards

'This book is for life, not just for Christmas! Packed with ideas about how to give a gift to the world, and rooted in scripture, this easy-to-read book has something for everyone, from eco-warriors to those just starting a green journey. Perfect for families, individuals, Eco Churches and groups.'
Debbie, David and Jamie Hawker, authors of *Changing the Climate* (BRF Ministries, 2021)

'Olivia's book offers a rare and wonderful moment when love of God, his word and his world all come together. Her reflections are thought-provoking and her advice accessible. I would recommend to anyone wanting to worship God afresh, through practical acts of love for his good creation at Christmas.'
Hannah Mann, environment programme manager, diocese of Oxford

'A wide-ranging, realistic and compassionate guide that includes reflective sections to feed your soul, and doesn't assume a one-size-fits-all solution. There's plenty here to get the eco-curious started, as well as ideas for those a bit further along in their sustainability journey. Many of the ideas can be taken forward into the rest of the year.'
Ruth Bancewicz, church engagement director, The Faraday Institute for Science and Religion, Cambridge

'Olivia's book helps us to think beyond a "White Christmas" and take steps towards a green, sustainable one. Full of hints to help you build new Christmas traditions that celebrate God's gift of life in Jesus and share it not only with family and friends but the whole planet. Don't just dream of a "Green Christmas" – begin to live it!'
Revd Dr Dave Gregory, Baptist minister and Missioner for Science and Environment

Make Christmas greener, one day at a time…

 Ministries

15 The Chambers, Vineyard
Abingdon OX14 3FE
+44 (0)1865 319700 | **brf.org.uk**

Bible Reading Fellowship (BRF) is a charity (233280)
and company limited by guarantee (301324),
registered in England and Wales

EU Authorised Representative: Easy Access System Europe –
Mustamäe tee 50, 10621 Tallinn, Estonia, **gpsr.requests@easproject.com**

ISBN 978 1 80039 430 8
First published 2025
10 9 8 7 6 5 4 3 2 1 0
All rights reserved

Text © Olivia Warburton 2025
This edition © Bible Reading Fellowship 2025
Cover and inside graphics © paolagio_photo/stock.adobe.com, © Tartila/stock.adobe.com, © Nur syifa fauziah/stock.adobe.com, © wendy14/stock.adobe.com, © portarefortuna/stock.adobe.com; © OpenClipart-Vectorson/pixabay.com

The author asserts the moral right to be identified as the author of this work

Acknowledgements

Unless otherwise acknowledged, scripture quotations are taken from The Holy Bible, New International Version (Anglicised edition) copyright © 1979, 1984, 2011 by Biblica. Used by permission of Hodder & Stoughton Publishers, a Hachette UK company. All rights reserved. 'NIV' is a registered trademark of Biblica. UK trademark number 1448790.

Every effort has been made to trace and contact copyright owners for material used in this resource. We apologise for any inadvertent omissions or errors, and would ask those concerned to contact us so that full acknowledgement can be made in the future.

A catalogue record for this book is available from the British Library

Printed and bound by in the UK by Zenith Media NP4 0DQ

Includes 111 eco-tips

Olivia Warburton

Dreaming of a *Green* Christmas

Sustainability and creation care for busy people

BRF
Ministries

A huge thank you to all the wonderful people, both local and further afield, who have offered ideas, encouragement and feedback for this project.

Photocopying for churches

Please report to CLA Church Licence any photocopy you make from this publication. Your church administrator or secretary will know who manages your CLA Church Licence.

The information you need to provide to your CLA Church Licence administrator is as follows:

Title, Author, Publisher and ISBN

If your church doesn't hold a CLA Church Licence, information about obtaining one can be found at **uk.ccli.com**

 # *This book will:*

- ✔ Help you navigate Advent and Christmas more sustainably and with less stress

- ✔ Give you 111 easy, practical eco-tips to reduce, reuse, recycle and generally go greener

- ✔ Recap the spiritual principles relating to creation care and why it's important

- ✔ Include 'Take a break' reflective moments focused on God's love for creation

- ✔ Kickstart positive, manageable habits that can be taken forward into the new year

Contents

STEP 1: GETTING READY............12

STEP 2: GETTING GOING............24

STEP 3: PICK-AND-MIX IDEAS....30

    Declutter.......................... 32

    Clean..............................32

    Christmas tree................... 33

    Decorations 34

Take a break ①...................... 35

    Christmas lights................ 37

    Advent calendar................ 37

    Christmas stockings........... 38

    Christmas cards 39

Take a break ②..................... 40

    Present buying 42

    Present wrapping.............. 45

    Trips and travelling............ 46

    Entertaining..................... 48

Take a break ③..................... 49

    Clothes 51

    Food 52

    Food waste 54

    Energy............................. 55

Take a break ④ 57
- Rest and exercise 59
- Nature 60
- Charity and community 61
- Recycling 62

Take a break ⑤ 64

Reflect, celebrate and breathe ... 66
Next steps 67
Resources and links 68

Appendix I: 20 sustainability shockers 72

Appendix II: 20 ways to break the bias 75

Wouldn't it be great if we could make Christmas greener, less wasteful, less stressful and more enjoyable, and have more space to focus on what it's really all about?

Well, I think we can.

STEP 1: GETTING READY

Underpinning it all...

the strange little story of the widow's offering.

As Jesus looked up, he saw the rich putting their gifts into the temple treasury. He also saw a poor widow put in two very small copper coins. 'Truly I tell you,' he said, 'this poor widow has put in more than all the others. All these people gave their gifts out of their wealth; but she out of her poverty put in all she had to live on.'

LUKE 21:1–4

Mindset shift

It's easy to think that whatever we do won't really make a difference, but this story says otherwise. So we don't have much time/energy/money/expertise? So climate change, let alone the world's many other problems, seems too big to make a dent in? In God's economy, even the smallest things count and have value.

This book is not about creating headaches or inducing a sense of guilt. Somehow, whenever the environment is mentioned, it's easy to feel overwhelmed and that we should be perfectly green in every part of our lives… and if we can't do that, we should just give up now. The story of the widow's offering shows us that small is beautiful and that condemnation has no part to play here.

Can't do everything? Of course we can't, nobody can. Let's think about it this way instead: 'I can't do that. But I could do THIS.'

Sustainability – the explainer

If you're reading this, hopefully you're on board with the general idea of sustainability and creation care. But other people in your life may not be, so the next few pages could be useful for explaining it to them. This also applies if you're a teacher, children's or youth leader or anyone else in a leadership role.

A ground rule as we begin: 'sustainability' here primarily refers to lifestyle and behaviour changes for the sake of the planet. But emotional and physical sustainability are crucial too. Actions need to be manageable to avoid discouragement or burnout further down the line. It's all about commonsense choices and, yes, some compromises.

Why is it so important?

The earth is the Lord's, and everything in it, the world, and all who live in it.
PSALM 24:1

Caring for our world shouldn't be a controversial idea. Taking care of something makes it last longer and run better. This is the planet we've got, and we need to look after it properly – to avoid draining its resources and to try to reverse some of the damage we've already done. So 'care' is a no-brainer. For Christians, the Bible says that God created the earth, loves it and wants us to take care of it. That's how we arrive at the idea of 'creation care'.

Some Christians over the centuries have struggled with this idea. Genesis 1:28 says that God told humans to 'fill the earth and subdue it. Rule over the fish in the sea and the birds in the sky and over every living creature that moves on the ground.' Some people along the way interpreted this to mean 'do what you like, you're in charge, there are no consequences'. But Genesis 2:15 clearly says, 'The Lord God took the man and put him in the Garden of Eden to work it and take care of it.' Yes, we can use the planet's resources, but this has to go alongside looking after it. It's about stewardship, not exploitation.

Certain parts of the church have seen creation care as a distraction from evangelism. Others have been nervous that it's a slippery slope that leads to people worshipping nature as God. But in the earliest centuries AD, the Celtic Christians completely understood that God loves creation, that the world around us speaks of God's glory and that being in harmony with nature isn't something to be suspicious of. When we care for the world around us, we are honouring God by showing respect for God's handiwork.

Not only that: caring for nature means caring for people. In Matthew 22:36–39 someone asked Jesus:

> 'Teacher, which is the greatest commandment in the Law?'
>
> Jesus replied: '"Love the Lord your God with all your heart and with all your soul and with all your mind." This is the first and greatest commandment. And the second is like it: "Love your neighbour as yourself."'

Living lightly on this planet isn't purely an environmental issue; it's a social justice issue. Loving our neighbour means thinking about how our actions affect other people. Fighting climate change is one way that we can have a lasting impact both on future generations and on people living today in all corners of the earth. When people's crops die because of drought or their homes are flooded or destroyed in wildfires, or rising temperatures cause heat-related illness and disease, we have a responsibility to do whatever we can to help, and to try to stop it happening.

This book doesn't offer a detailed explanation of the science. Stats are updated so continually that it's best to go online to get the latest figures. At the back (see page 68) you'll find some helpful links that can give you the context you need.

However, to list some key areas of concern:

 Devastating climate events are becoming more frequent and more violent all around the world.

 Natural habitats are being destroyed, with many plant and animal species already extinct or in danger of extinction. Agriculture is a primary cause of deforestation and biodiversity loss.

 Plastic pollution in our water systems is harming fish, wildlife and plant life. Human health is also affected as we ingest microplastics.

 As temperatures rise, there are other significant effects on public health, such as infectious diseases spreading more rapidly, increased risk of heat-related illness and underlying medical conditions being exacerbated.

But it's so hard...

It's certainly not straightforward. Environmental action requires change and not everyone wants that, so there's a fair amount of misinformation to combat, not to mention greenwashing. It's important to be savvy and do your research on companies to check out their claims, because sometimes people want to look like they're trying harder than they are. And then, let's admit that environmental news can frequently be negative and depressing! The positive stories get drowned out – so prayer and a hopeful attitude are essential.

Change is happening, globally and locally. And as with any trend, the more people get on board, the more momentum builds. There are lots of things that we can all do, many of which may even save us money or be healthier for us. An eco-swap may not be perfect, but if it's better than the alternative, it's worth doing. And the more something becomes a habit, the easier it is.

The usual suspects: some blockers and myths

'Anything I do as an individual doesn't really make a difference.'
Please don't ever think your contribution doesn't matter. Remember the story of the widow's offering and notice what Jesus *didn't* say: 'Well, I don't know why she bothered, that's not going to help much!' It shouldn't all be on the individual, of course, despite the messaging from large corporations with vested interests, but we do each have a part to play. What we choose to do (or not do) does matter and does help shift the dial.

'We're not the worst offenders.'
It's tempting to look at other individuals, communities, companies or nations and feel that they should take the lead in cleaning up. But we have all sinned and fallen short of the glory of God, and in God's world we are all connected. We are still responsible for what we consume, even if another country has manufactured it. It can never be 'somebody else's problem'.

'Green solutions aren't perfect.'
Well, no. But they are less damaging and more beneficial longer term than continuing as we are, and they're getting better all the time as more companies invest in them.

'It's too expensive.'
Green technology costs are falling rapidly, green jobs are on the rise and clean energy is reliably predicted to save trillions. Perhaps it feels more expensive for me as an individual right now. But some eco-swaps such as bulk buying and refill options can work out cheaper and save time too. Think in terms of small incremental changes rather than switching out everything at once. And with the climate impacts we're already seeing, can we really afford not to take action?

'It's such a sacrifice.'
Some things probably will feel less convenient initially or take some getting used to. But there may be other benefits to offset this, such as improved health from adopting a more plant-based diet, or the sense of freedom that comes from having less stuff to look after. And it's never as difficult as it might seem to adjust to a new normal.

'I don't have time.'
Researching new products or simply finding the headspace to change habits and routines can feel just too much. Again, starting with one or two changes and building up little by little gives the best chance of success. And Christmas is a great time to experiment!

How and when to use this book

Start using this book before Christmas, the earlier the better, to give plenty of time to get ready (which is always a good idea, whether you're trying to be sustainable or not!). But depending on when you lay your hands on a copy, do as much or as little as you can manage. Jump to a particular section if you like – this book doesn't have to be worked through page by page. Tick off tips as you complete them, and don't feel that you have to do everything. This isn't about adding stress to an already stressful season. It's about feeling better about how you're approaching it all, and hopefully having some fun with the new ideas too. Some ideas are general ones which can be taken forward into the new year. Then pull out the book next Christmas and tick off a few more! Whatever you're able to do will make a difference.

The **Take a break** sections are just that – you can turn to them whenever you feel you need a moment to pause, reflect, recharge and remember why the choice you're making to care for creation is so important. Each one offers a bite-sized reflection on a short Bible passage, and you'll find them dotted throughout the ideas section.

You can use this book on your own, with your family, or with another group that you're responsible for. The star icon indicates activities that may work well with younger children, depending of course on specific ages and situations.

    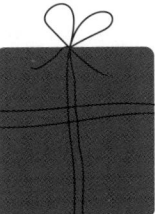

STEP 2: GETTING GOING

Principles and preparation

Key principle ① Psalm 24:1

'**T**he earth is the Lord's, and everything in it, the world, and all who live in it.'

Meaning? God cares about stuff. Physical, practical things. Everyday life choices. Nothing is too small or unimportant. And the amazing thing is, one thing leads to another! One small step feels good and creates a little bit of momentum for the next small step.

But first let's take stock.

Think about these questions:

① What things immediately come to mind that you'd like to do differently this Christmas?

② Talk about what's stopping you doing them. Time? Energy? Money? Do you know what 'different' looks like yet, or not really?

③ Who do you want to spend time with over Christmas? Which relationships are most important to invest in? Are there any where you feel obliged or guilty? Acknowledge this and explore if there are ways to reduce the pressure.

Use the space on the opposite page to note down your ideas and thoughts.

Step 2: getting going 27

Key principle ② Matthew 6:26

> '*Look at the birds of the air; they do not sow or reap or store away in barns, and yet your heavenly Father feeds them.*'

Meaning? Don't worry about money. BUT it is important to be clear about how much you have available. From there, work out what you *need* to spend and what you'd *like* to spend.

What's most important to you at Christmas? What do you most enjoy, or find most fulfilling and worthwhile? Is it the food, entertaining, seeing family, presents, going to a church service? What are the non-negotiables? If you had to compromise on something, what would it be? Once you've worked through all this, you can remind yourself of those priorities whenever decisions need to be made. It may help to write them down and put them somewhere you'll keep seeing them.

Think 'reduce, reuse, recycle'. Reduce is generally the place to start. What do you simply not need to buy, or do? What choices are perhaps causing stress, worry or financial pressure for yourself or others? MoneySavingExpert Martin Lewis comments:

'Done right, gifts can create real warmth, but it's time to realise that, done wrong, it can hurt more than it helps. Perhaps the real gift is to release someone from the obligation of buying you a present?'*

Try to identify at least one thing that you're just not going to invest in this Christmas. Free up time and resources for your real priorities.

Now write down some family commitments or aspirations. Nothing is too small or boring – remember the widow's offering!

We commit to…
We'll try our best to…
We'd like to move towards…
We're not going to…
Whatever else, we will…
We're making a note that next year we want to…

Now we're ready to begin!

*moneysavingexpert.com/2009/11/is-it-time-to-ban-christmas-presents

STEP 3: PICK-AND-MIX IDEAS

Take a few minutes to skim through the ideas that follow, and make a note of the ones you'd like to try. This should counter any feelings of overwhelm and give you a manageable plan. Activities that younger children can get involved with are marked with a star, but please assess each activity carefully as to whether it is safe for individual children and adapt as needed.

Tick off each idea as you complete it, so that you can see and be encouraged by the changes you're making.

    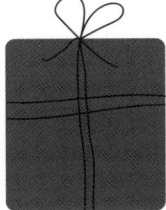

Declutter

 Some level of Christmas-generated clutter is unavoidable, so creating a bit of extra space beforehand will help reduce the pressure. Set a stopwatch and whizz round the house to locate anything you don't need or want anymore. There will be some easy wins. Many hands make light work – partner up or target different rooms. Recycle, donate or sell the items you're parting with. For younger children, make it a treasure hunt! ☐

Clean

 Look for eco-friendly brands and refillable or reusable products. Some options to consider are recycled loo roll, washable bamboo kitchen roll (lasts way longer than paper) and bar soap (avoids the plastic packaging of liquid soap). ☐

 Instead of using disposable wipes for kitchen and bathroom surfaces, cut up old T-shirts to make wipes or dusters. ☐

- Reduce chemicals and save some money by making your own cleaning products. Lemon juice, white vinegar and water make a good basic multipurpose cleaner. Add bicarbonate of soda for a deeper clean, such as removing limescale. Quick and easy recipes can be found online. ☐

Christmas tree

- Rent a Christmas tree which can be returned to be replanted. ☐

- If you can't rent, buy a potted spruce with roots that you can plant out to reuse each year. ☐

- Alternatively, buy a Grown in Britain or FSC-certified tree to ensure that it's from a well-managed forest, and recycle it properly. Most councils recycle trees by turning them into chippings, reducing the carbon footprint by up to 80% compared with sending them to landfill. Check your local council website for details of their collection service. ☐

- The carbon footprint of a new plastic tree is significantly higher than for a real tree, and it will end up in landfill. But if you already have one, keep it for as long as possible – they can last for years. ☐

Decorations

- Tinsel and baubles are not recyclable. Use those you already have, but don't buy more! ☐

- Make your own decorations from recyclable materials, such as dried orange slice ornaments, sticks of cinnamon, loo roll fairies or giant paper snowflakes. Turn scrap paper into paper chains. Foraged materials like pine cones and holly can be used for wreaths, which can then be recycled at the kerbside. ☐

- Buy or make one special tree decoration each year. ☐

Take a break ❶

> '**D**o not store up for yourselves treasures on earth, where moths and vermin destroy, and where thieves break in and steal. But store up for yourselves treasures in heaven, where moths and vermin do not destroy, and where thieves do not break in and steal. For where your treasure is, there your heart will be also.'
> MATTHEW 6:19–21

Everywhere we look, there are books, blogs and TV programmes advising us how we can declutter. It's a very practical principle, which promotes our physical well-being as we make the spaces we live in more user-friendly, manageable and attractive, and which reduces the amount of stuff we have to spend time and energy looking after. But did you realise that it's a spiritual principle too?

We all have attachments. But if we're too attached to other things, it stands to reason that this will start to affect our attachment to God, our parent figure and caregiver. As Jesus puts it: 'Where your treasure is, there your heart will be also.'

Are we too attached to a particular lifestyle, or how other people perceive us?

What do we feel we couldn't live without? Why is that? And is it getting in the way of our relationship with God, and others?

    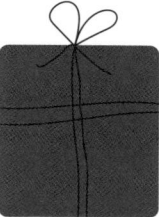

Christmas lights

- Outdoor Christmas lights look lovely, but they create light pollution and cost the UK millions per day over the festive period, so could you scale back? Turn them off when you're not in and overnight. Use a timer to make this easier. ☐

- Switch to LED lights, which use up to 80% less energy. Consider solar-powered LEDs if you have solar panels. ☐

- Recycle broken or damaged Christmas lights – wires can be recycled at the kerbside and batteries at the supermarket. Remove any bulbs and dispose of these separately at your nearest recycling centre. ☐

Advent calendar

> Instead of an Advent calendar, light an Advent candle each day. ☐

Create a 'reverse Advent calendar': each day through Advent, put a food item aside in a box and then donate it all to a local food bank. (You may want to finish this earlier than Christmas Day, as donating before Christmas will be appreciated for those who can't afford treats or even essentials.) ☐

 Set up a 'kindness calendar', which suggests a kind action per day through Advent – for everyone to take part in! Templates can be found online to print off, or you could create a personalised, whole-family-approved version. ☐

 If a traditional Advent calendar is essential, buy or make a reusable fabric one. Fill it with fair-trade chocolates or homemade treats. ☐

Christmas stockings

 Christmas stockings can be a real challenge. Rather than resorting to uninspired fillers that aren't wanted or needed, include items that you would have bought anyway, like socks, fair-trade edibles and gifts that you know in advance the recipient will definitely like or use! ☐

Replace the Christmas stocking ritual with one where presents or chocolates are hidden around the house, with or without clues, for a Christmas morning treasure hunt. ☐

Christmas cards

 Only send a card if you're planning to write a personal message inside, and/or only to relatives who would really appreciate a paper card. ☐

 Choose cards made from recycled paper, ones that display the FSC or PEFC logo to show they come from sustainably managed forests, plantable cards or e-cards (but be aware that digital has a carbon footprint too). Look for vegan inks and suppliers who use renewable energy. ☐

 Avoid cards with foil, plastic film or glitter. They're unrecyclable and the glitter can end up anywhere, including in our water systems. ☐

 Recycle any cards that you receive, or cut them up to use for gift tags next year. ☐

Take a break ❷

'*You are the salt of the earth. But if the salt loses its saltiness, how can it be made salty again? It is no longer good for anything, except to be thrown out and trampled underfoot. You are the light of the world. A town built on a hill cannot be hidden. Neither do people light a lamp and put it under a bowl. Instead they put it on its stand, and it gives light to everyone in the house. In the same way, let your light shine before others, that they may see your good deeds and glorify your Father in heaven.*'

MATTHEW 5:13–16

A while back, I came across the concept of two-minute habits. We all struggle with New Year's resolutions, don't we? Creating a good habit is so much harder than creating a bad one. But doing something for just two minutes a day sets the bar so low that you have a much better chance of clearing it! As in fitness or diet, so in spiritual matters. We can train to be saltier, to give more light, little by little. And the training never really stops – there's always another small step we can take.

It's also worth remembering that physical, mental, emotional and spiritual tend to be far more interconnected than we often think. God loves us mind, body and spirit, and cares about everything about us. Being 'salt and light' involves material, practical lifestyle choices: how we spend or invest our money, what we eat, how we travel and how we vote. All of these things impact other people in this global community we're part of, and Jesus calls us to love our neighbour as ourselves.

    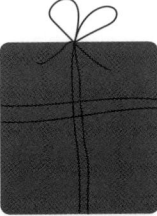

Present buying

 Reduce the number of presents bought – perhaps a simple food or drink gift for each adult, with more personalised gifts for children. Or opt for a Secret Santa (online sites take the stress out of organising this) where each person, or the group, gets a more meaningful gift, rather than lots of cheap ones. Note that for this to work, you will need to have the conversation in good time, before other people get going with their present buying! ☐

 For children, select presents from the following categories: something they really want; something they need; something to wear; something to read; something to eat; something to share; something to do; a special surprise. ☐

 Ask people what they would really like for Christmas. Ideally they will give you a few ideas to choose from. Children can write a wish list, and help with interrogating other family members! ☐

- If you're thinking of opening a savings account or junior ISA for a child at Christmas, or know that relatives have this in mind, opt for a fossil-fuel-free bank or ethical ISA. ☐

- Actively search for sustainable brands and eco-friendly products, but if you don't actually need something, don't be tempted to buy things, however 'eco' or however much of a bargain! Focus on buying less and buying ethically. ☐

- Buy second-hand from charity shops or online marketplaces. Second-hand gifts, refurbished technology and so on will always be a lower-carbon option, because you're making the most of the energy and resources that have already gone into a product, and potentially saving something from landfill. ☐

- Avoid buying cheap, disposable gifts, particularly anything made of plastic. One or two higher-quality items may well work out cheaper, too, than lots of smaller fillers. ☐

> ⭐ Give homemade gifts, such as cookies, hot chocolate bombs, truffles, jams or chutneys, herbal teas, body scrub or handcrafted items. Or make something personalised and creative, such as a word cloud which you could print and frame. ☐

- Give experiences instead of physical gifts. This can include tickets to events, afternoon tea, memberships or homemade vouchers offering a meal out or something the person would appreciate having done for them. Even quite young children enjoy the idea of a day out, especially if the tickets are wrapped in an interesting fashion. ☐

- Sometimes cash (or a bank transfer) may be the most appreciated present, particularly by older teens. It may be 'boring' for you, but not for them! ☐

- If you buy new, try to support small local businesses (don't forget to take your reusable shopping bags). Shop local for last-minute purchases. ☐

- If researching gifts online, use an ethical search engine such as Ecosia, and search 'ethical, fair trade and handmade gifts'. ☐

- If buying toiletries, choose ones in metal tins or glass jars instead of plastic bottles or tubes. ☐

- Give plants rather than cut flowers. ☐

Step 3: pick-and-mix ideas 45

🌲 Present-giving and receiving can be a cause of significant anxiety for some. If this is the case, stress could be reduced by an agreement that everyone buys themselves the present they would like and shows it to each other on Christmas Day. ☐

🎄 Re-gift any unwanted presents you receive. ☐

Present wrapping

⭐ Use up any gift wrap left over from last year. Remember that if it's covered in plastic film, foil or glitter it won't be recyclable, so don't buy any more once it's used up! The same goes for tissue paper. ☐

⭐ Use recycled, compostable and recyclable wrapping paper or brown paper. ☐

⭐ Plastic sticky tape is not recyclable. Use ribbon, string or paper tape instead. ☐

⭐ Go tape-free with *furoshiki* and wrap gifts in fabric. ☐

Reduce waste further by buying gifts with little or no packaging. Shopping local can help, especially if you have a refill shop nearby. ☐

⭐ Make gift tags from last year's Christmas cards, or create your own unique artwork! ☐

Trips and travelling

 Think carefully about your travel plans over the Christmas season and whether every trip is essential. Are there any car journeys you could swap out, particularly short local ones? ☐

⭐ Rather than booking expensive day trips, particularly if you have younger children, plan free, home-based activities such as a family film with hot chocolate, reading Christmas-themed books from the library or camping out under the Christmas tree. ☐

 While tricky if you have family abroad, do your best to avoid air travel, particularly short flights. Try taking the train within the UK or to Europe. (Travelling to France by Eurostar rather than flying, for example, reduces the journey's carbon footprint by 96%.) ☐

Step 3: pick-and-mix ideas 47

 If you are flying, offset your carbon footprint via a scheme such as Climate Stewards. ☐

 Walk whenever you can, use public transport or share lifts wherever possible. ☐

 If driving, clear out the car boot before you travel to ensure you're not carrying excess weight, and try to fit all your luggage inside the car – roof boxes add to drag, meaning you'll burn more fuel. ☐

 Drive at the most fuel-efficient speed and take the most fuel-efficient route. If you can, avoid the busiest travel times, saving fuel burned sitting in traffic jams. ☐

 En route, take your reusable mug and travel cutlery with you. Avoid over-packaged meals to go and single-use cups. You can sometimes get discounts on drinks by bringing your own cup. ☐

 If you're booking holidays for next year, browse eco-tourism websites and enjoy researching the best possible sustainable break! ☐

Entertaining

- Think creatively – do you really need to host a large party? Sometimes a simpler gathering or arranging to meet up at a café or pub might be just as much fun and saves resources. ☐

- If guests will be bringing food, avoid duplication and waste by creating a list to capture who has signed up for what. ☐

- Avoid disposable plates, cups and cutlery. Hire glasses if needed, and save water by fully loading the dishwasher rather than hand washing. ☐

- Use washable material tablecloths and napkins rather than single-use plastic or paper ones. ☐

> ⭐ Buy plastic-free and/or FSC-certified crackers, or reusable 'fill your own' crackers. Alternatively, make them from loo rolls and wrapping paper, or go cracker-free altogether! ☐

- Encourage people to take food home, and provide reusable containers. ☐

Take a break ❸

'*Therefore I tell you, do not worry about your life, what you will eat or drink; or about your body, what you will wear. Is not life more than food, and the body more than clothes? Look at the birds of the air; they do not sow or reap or store away in barns, and yet your heavenly Father feeds them… And why do you worry about clothes? See how the flowers of the field grow. They do not labour or spin. Yet I tell you that not even Solomon in all his splendour was dressed like one of these.*'
MATTHEW 6:25–26, 28–29

One thing I notice about Jesus in the gospels is that he lives free. He isn't held back by worrying about what people think of him, or by being afraid of offending people. He doesn't let his own family direct his actions or tell him what to do, although he treats them with respect. He takes time out from ministering to the crowds when he needs to. He gives generously of himself, but is no people pleaser. He embodies love, but there are no unhelpful attachments to get in the way. And he doesn't seem to worry about the practicalities of everyday life.

I don't think that this was effortless – Jesus was fully human, after all. So it's an example we can try to follow. Being ready to try to wean ourselves off anything that is holding us back from being the people that we can be – free, joyful children of God.

    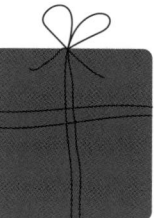

Clothes

- ⭐ Dressing for the party season starts with 'shopping your wardrobe'. See exactly what you already have and whether you actually need anything else. ☐

- 🎄 If you do need to buy more clothes, check out charity or vintage shops, a clothes swap event or pre-loved websites. You can also rent outfits and accessories. ☐

- 🎄 Re-wear last year's Christmas jumper, buy one from a charity shop or swap with a friend. ☐

- 🎄 Swap or do a call-out for nativity costumes via local online forums or school chat groups, or pick up something second-hand. ☐

- 🎄 Make use of local services for mending or alterations to repurpose an outfit – these are also often a more affordable option. ☐

🌲 If you're buying new, avoid synthetic fibres such as polyester and acrylic in favour of bamboo, organic cotton or recycled materials. Go as ethical as you can afford, and fair trade if possible. Check the retailer's environmental credentials on the Ethical Consumer website to avoid being greenwashed. ☐

 Wash clothing at 30 degrees on a short cycle and air dry (much cheaper and greener than a tumble dryer). Consider investing in a dehumidifier if damp is an issue. Try to increase the number of wears between washes – clothes will last longer if washed less often! Use non-biological washing powder or liquid, an eco egg or laundry sheets. ☐

Food

 Buy LOAF where possible: **L**ocally produced, **O**rganically grown, **A**nimal friendly, **F**airly traded. ☐

 Check labels and logos. Look for UK seasonal produce to reduce food miles and support UK farmers, and sustainability certifications such as RSPO-certified palm oil and MSC-certified seafood. ☐

- ⭐ Find out online which producers are growing food using nature-friendly farming systems and supporting local sustainable agriculture (see websites on page 68). ☐

- ⭐ Move as far as you possibly can towards a plant-based diet, saving meat as a treat. You could start by cutting out particularly carbon-intensive meats like beef and lamb. Reduce dairy – maybe switch out milk for a plant alternative like oat, alongside moderate cheese and yoghurt consumption. If you are able to, give it a try! Remember that a new habit will always take a little while to feel natural. ☐

- 🌲 If eating meat, go local, organic and free-range, and prioritise quality over quantity. ☐

- 🌲 Buy drinks locally and seasonally – avoid citrus and summer fruits at this time of year. ☐

- ⭐ Try buying loose fruit and veg to cut down on single-use soft plastics. Challenge: count how many pieces of plastic food packaging you get through in a week. ☐

Food waste

⭐ First, check the cupboards – what food or drink needs using up? ☐

🎄 Make a meal plan for Christmas week. Work out how leftovers can be built into this and include some simpler dishes too. This will free up time and increase everyone's appreciation of the more special meals when they come. ☐

🎄 Who are you cooking for? If some people have dietary needs or preferences (such as being vegetarian), cook a single dish that everyone will enjoy eating, rather than having multiple options (such as meat and non-meat) and increasing the cooking. ☐

🎄 If you have time, prep and freeze some meals in advance. ☐

⭐ If you have the flexibility, wait until just before Christmas and see what supermarkets are getting rid of at the last minute. ☐

🎄 Freeze any leftovers, or use airtight containers and beeswax wraps if eating them in the near future. ☐

- ⭐ Donate excess food via food banks, local shelters or community apps, or share with neighbours. This also gives an excuse for a short walk! ☐

- 🎄 If you can't find another home for the food, make sure you're using your food waste and compost bins correctly. Check that you're composting everything that you can. ☐

- ⭐ Turn appropriate leftover food into beauty products. Avocado, banana, cucumber and yoghurt all make great face masks. ☐

Energy

- 🎄 Use a slow cooker, microwave or air fryer for smaller meals instead of your oven. Plan ahead so that if the oven is on, it's full. ☐

- 🎄 Heat the person: turn the thermostat down a degree or two and keep warm with extra layers of clothing and blankets or heated throws. ☐

Challenge: make a note every time you use water over the course of a day. What can you do to use less? Don't run the tap when brushing your teeth. Make your shower one minute shorter. Only fill the kettle to the amount you need. ☐

 Ensure that lights are only switched on when necessary and buy energy-saving LED light bulbs. Create a family habit of turning off lights when leaving a room. ☐

 Unplug Christmas lights, the TV and other electronics when not in use to avoid phantom energy consumption. Don't leave your phone on charge all night – it only needs a couple of hours. ☐

 Christmas is a good time for a digital detox. It's easy to forget that every email, online search or streamed video uses energy. Unsubscribe from marketing newsletters; avoid sending unnecessary attachments; and maybe find a few minutes' downtime to delete files and photos that are taking up space on your computer or phone. ☐

Take a break ❹

> **H**ow lovely is your dwelling-place, Lord Almighty! My soul yearns, even faints, for the courts of the Lord; my heart and my flesh cry out for the living God. Even the sparrow has found a home, and the swallow a nest for herself, where she may have her young – a place near your altar, Lord Almighty, my King and my God. Blessed are those who dwell in your house; they are ever praising you.
>
> PSALM 84:1–4

Psalm 84 is full of delightful promises for those who rest in God's presence. We will be blessed. We will be ever praising God. Streams of living water will flow from us. We will go from strength to strength. We will receive favour and honour. No good thing is withheld from those who trust in God. Better is one day in God's courts than a thousand elsewhere.

But how do we rest? Even if we are well-rested physically, are our minds ever truly at rest? In Matthew 11:28, Jesus says, 'Come to me, all you who are weary and burdened, and I will give you rest.' That's not just physical.

It's worth thinking about the burdens we each find it hard to bring to our heavenly Father, and the behaviours that may be getting in the way of true rest.

The psalm ends, 'Lord Almighty, blessed is the one who trusts in you.' In trusting God with our anxieties, our fears, our frustrations and our pain, we can find rest.

    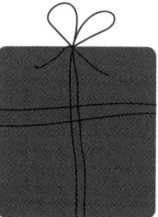

Rest and exercise

- ⭐ Both rest and exercise can be hard to find time for over Christmas, and both are really important to maintain. As a family, talk about what you each feel you need so that you can support each other to achieve this. ☐

- ⭐ Walk around the local neighbourhood after dark to admire the lights and the Advent window displays. ☐

- ⭐ A Boxing Day walk is a great tradition, but also build in exercise 'snacks' throughout the holiday season. A great habit to take into the new year! ☐

- ⭐ Experiment with the two-minute rule – choose something to do for just two minutes per day and start doing it. It's an easy way to form a new habit. ☐

- ⭐ Music can help both with exercising and with being able to rest. Create a Christmas playlist of your most energising or relaxing tunes. They don't have to be Christmas-themed… unless you want them to be! ☐

- ⭐ Plan a social media detox for however long you feel you can manage, or restrict the amount of time you spend on certain platforms. Share your intentions with someone who will help you stay accountable. ☐

Nature

- ⭐ Take a walk around your local park or nature reserve and do some bird-spotting, or head to the woods to pick up pine cones. You could use the time to pray, on your own or as a family, or simply enjoy God's creation. ☐

- ⭐ If the weather is too bad to go outside, watch nature films or documentaries for an inspiring alternative. Older teens could do some armchair volunteering identifying animal species on the citizen science platform Zooniverse. ☐

⭐ Look after your local environment and the creatures in it – pick up litter and put out bird food. ☐

⭐ Make a bird feeder. Tie ribbon, string or wire to a large pine cone, dip the cone in melted lard or a vegetarian alternative, and roll it in bird seed, peanut butter and raisins until it is thoroughly coated. ☐

🎄 Plan your garden or window boxes for next year. Could you grow herbs or vegetables, or plant bee-friendly wildflowers? ☐

Charity and community

⭐ Shift the focus: chat as a family about how you can give as well as receive this Christmas. ☐

⭐ Pick a charity or community initiative to support by volunteering, signing a campaign or petition, or making a Christmas donation as a family. ☐

⭐ When you do your Christmas grocery shopping, buy a few extra items to take to your local food bank. ☐

⭐ Think who might appreciate being invited round for a meal or being given a gift, or get involved with a Christmas meal for the lonely or homeless. ☐

⭐ Become Christmas 'angels' and do some random acts of kindness. ☐

Recycling

🎄 Check your council website to see what they will and won't accept for recycling. Make sure you're completely clear on what can be recycled and where – it's not always obvious! ☐

⭐ Remove any sticky tape from wrapping paper. Paper with glitter on it, or that is metallic or has a plastic film, can't be recycled and needs to go into the black bin. The same applies to cards. ☐

Step 3: pick-and-mix ideas 63

⭐ Make foil easier to collect by scrunching it into a ball about the size of a tennis ball. ☐

⭐ If you're recycling shredded paper, put it inside an old envelope to keep it all together. ☐

🎄 Look out for opportunities at events and other people's houses to take away recycling if it looks as if it will otherwise go into landfill. ☐

    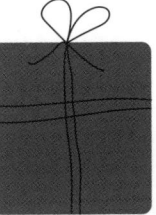

Take a break 5

> *After Jesus was born in Bethlehem in Judea, during the time of King Herod, Magi from the east came to Jerusalem and asked, 'Where is the one who has been born king of the Jews? We saw his star when it rose and have come to worship him'... After they had heard the king, they went on their way, and the star they had seen when it rose went ahead of them until it stopped over the place where the child was. When they saw the star, they were overjoyed. On coming to the house, they saw the child with his mother Mary, and they bowed down and worshipped him. Then they opened their treasures and presented him with gifts of gold, frankincense and myrrh.*
> MATTHEW 2:1–2, 9–11

Sometimes extravagant celebration is appropriate. These 'magi' (scholars who may have been male or female) travelled a long way, bringing luxury gifts for the baby Jesus. They know what's important. Half-hearted worship isn't really worship at all.

When he grew up, Jesus' first miracle was turning water into top-quality wine at a wedding. Later, he commended a woman who anointed him liberally with expensive perfume, an action which others saw as wasteful and misdirected. In all our careful stewardship of resources, let's try not to judge others or become legalistic and anxious. Let's live as lightly on this planet as we can. But where we need to invest resources to bless others, let's do so freely and joyfully, as the magi did.

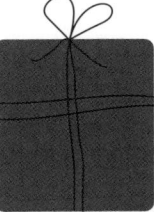

Reflect, celebrate... and breathe!

Making sustainable changes isn't always easy, and at Christmas time it can be especially challenging to navigate a path through family dynamics and societal expectations. Progress may seem slow, but any changes you've made will have been worth it and will have made a difference.

Take a moment to reflect on your family Christmas:

 What changes did we make?

 What new things did we try?

 What did we learn?

 What are we going to remember for next year?

 # *Next steps*

Go back to the list you made at the beginning (p. 27) and look at some of the longer-term aspirations. If you feel ready for it, map out the next steps towards these, whether that's making a switch to green energy or moving towards more ethical finances across your banking, mortgage or pension. Set aside little, manageable chunks of time to start exploring and researching, and think about what a realistic timescale could look like.

And meanwhile, keep decluttering. One thing in, one out. It's easier than it sounds, and it weakens the hold that 'stuff' can have on us. Jesus talked so much about our attitude to money and possessions, it's clear that he saw it as a spiritual issue – both in terms of loving our neighbour and the world we live in, and because of the freedom that holding these things lightly can bring us, helping us draw closer to the one who uniquely lived free.

Let's make next year simpler and more sustainable still.

Resources and links

Here are some resources and links you might find helpful – of course there are many more!

Environmental science

 bbc.co.uk/news/science-environment-24021772

 science.nasa.gov/climate-change/what-is-climate-change

 un.org/en/climatechange/science/causes-effects-climate-change

 natgeokids.com/uk/discover/geography/general-geography/what-is-climate-change

 bbc.com/future/article/20200305-why-your-internet-habits-are-not-as-clean-as-you-think

❄ **waterbear.com** – free streaming service for environmental films and storytelling.

Environmental action

❄ **arocha.org** – global family of conservation organisations working together to live out God's calling to care for creation.

❄ **ecochurch.arocha.org.uk** – A Rocha UK's Eco Church programme equips churches in England and Wales to care for creation.

❄ **zooniverse.org/get-involved/volunteer** – citizen science platform including a range of environmental projects.

❄ **clientearth.org** – law charity fighting the world's largest polluters.

❄ **hubbub.org.uk** – runs creative lifestyle change campaigns for individuals, communities and businesses.

❄ **climatestewards.org** – helps people to measure, reduce and offset their carbon footprint.

Consumer research

- **ethicalconsumer.org** – ethical and eco shopping guides for more than 100 products and services.

- **products.impactscore.app** – shows sustainable products in UK supermarkets.

- **regenerativefarmersofuk.com/map** – shows small-scale producers growing food using nature-friendly farming systems.

- **bigbarn.co.uk** – shows locally produced food and drink in your area.

Food waste

- **lovefoodhatewaste.com**

- **thefullfreezer.com/canifreezeit**

- **olioapp.com/en**
- **toogoodtogo.com**

Pre-loved

- **vinted.co.uk** and **thrift.plus** – clothes.
- **lovedbefore.london** – toys.
- **wob.com** – books.

Travel

- **ecobnb.com** – find your sustainable accommodation.
- **seat61.com** – guide to train travel in the UK, Europe and worldwide.

Appendix 1:
20 sustainability shockers – which do we secretly relate to?

- Opting for single-use plastics because it's more convenient.

- Jumping in the car for a short journey.

- Focusing more on the amount of saturated fat in oat milk or whether it's UPF than the environmental wins.

- Attending to just about anything that's simpler to contemplate than the climate crisis (lots of choice there).

- Requiring a sustainability shift to be 100% perfect before adopting it. Only a 90% improvement? 'Guess I won't make the switch, then.'

Appendix 1: 20 sustainability shockers

- Dismissing creation care as an over-hyped distraction from more important issues.

- Choosing the first item that comes to hand at the supermarket.

- Living in the echo chamber of aligned opinions; it's so much easier.

- 'I don't have every piece of information about a possible eco-swap at my fingertips, so I'm not keen on it.'

- 'The status quo feels safer (and less effort) than doing something that might turn out to be worse.'

- Writing-off green technologies because they're complex to understand and have less of a track record.

- 'Any lifestyle changes I make are not going to make any difference to the climate crisis. Governments and big tech need to sort it out.'

- 'The planet is doomed, let's all just give up now!'

- Defending behaviours that are too important to our comfort to change. 'The airline's scheduling the plane to make the trip anyway…'

- Justifying things because 'we deserve it', 'everyone does it' or 'I would but it's too expensive.'

- Just feeling really guilty, overwhelmed and unable to cope.

- Accepting a company's claims on the label without question.

- 'You can't teach an old dog new tricks – I'm not going to change my habits now.'

- 'It's important to maintain the status quo: traditional solutions have always worked fine.'

- Picking a couple of eco actions and that's me done – #sorted #doingmybit.

Appendix 2:
20 ways to break the bias – which can we adopt?

- Research eco-friendly alternatives and see what's out there.
- Reduce waste where possible by repurposing or repairing.
- Question your assumptions and review your routines.
- Think bigger picture and don't let perfect be the enemy ofgood.
- Decide priorities upfront when making a purchase, so you don't get distracted.
- Try and identify the real blockers, and don't be afraid of complexity.

- Start small: decide what you are and aren't going to do something about. You can always build up.

- Work on forming good habits. Once they're habits, they take much less energy!

- Consciously seek out alternative voices, like trying out a different news feed.

- Change could be positive – familiar isn't always better.

- When you don't know the answer, get more information and see if that helps.

- Take a step back and think: is there an agenda being pushed here?

- Catch yourself coming up with objections. Are you looking for an excuse to opt out?

- Feel the pain – is your sense of dissatisfaction or discomfort flagging up something important?

- Be open to other people's opinions. They might just be on to something.

- Don't be afraid to change your mind. Inconsistency isn't a bad thing if you end up in a better place.

- If 'It's good enough' really means 'I'm in a hurry', slow down and take the time to do it properly.

- Trust your gut when purchasing. If you feel unsure or dissatisfied, something's not quite right.

- But avoid the paralysis of seeking the perfect product – it doesn't exist.

- Experiment, one little thing at a time, and it should get easier.

Explore the story of the first Christmas together as a family! *The Christmas Story* is written for parents, grandparents and carers to share with their children through an interactive family Bible and prayer time. Each section provides a brief comment on the passage, questions to discuss, a visual aid to encourage engagement with the story, an activity idea, a prayer idea, a key verse and an Old Testament story link.

The Christmas Story: for families to share
Readings, questions, activities and prayers
Martyn Payne
978 1 80039 120 8 £2.50

brfonline.org.uk

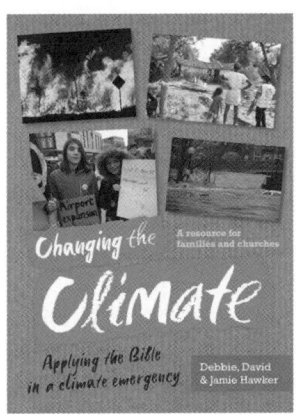

The climate crisis is one of the most important issues of our time, threatening lives and livelihoods. The Bible teaches us that God the creator put humans on the Earth to take care of it; to show love to all, and to care for the poor and vulnerable. This workbook shows how the Bible is relevant to environmentalism, and how we can all play our part in limiting the negative effects of climate change. Each chapter looks at a particular Bible passage, connects it with climate action, poses questions and suggests practical steps that can be taken.

Changing the Climate
Applying the Bible in a climate emergency
Debbie, David and Jamie Hawker
978 1 80039 022 5 £9.99

brfonline.org.uk

 Ministries

Inspiring people of all ages to grow in Christian faith

BRF Ministries is the home of Anna Chaplaincy, Living Faith, Messy Church and Parenting for Faith

As a charity, our work would not be possible without fundraising and gifts in wills. To find out more and to donate, visit brf.org.uk/give or call +44 (0)1235 462305